Jump and Shout

CHEERLEADING PRACTICE

TRACY NELSON MAURER

Rourke
Publishing LLC
Vero Beach, Florida 32964

Project Assistance courtesy of Jennifer Tell, Dance and Cheer Factory, Forest Lake, Minnesota.

The author also extends appreciation to Mike Maurer, Kendall and Lois Nelson, and the Rourke team. A special thank you to Jodi Belisle for her laughter, support, and amazing flexibility.

Photo Credits: Cover, pgs 4, 7, 16, 20, 21, 22, 25 ©PIR
Title, pgs 15, 26, 28, 38 ©PHOTOSPORT.COM
pg 9 ©USDA/Ken Hammond
pgs 32, 36, 37, 40, 41, 42 ©Paul Martinez/PHOTOSPORT.COM
pgs 14, 17, 30, 34, 43, 44 ©Peter Schlitt/PHOTOSPORT.COM

Editor: Frank Sloan

Cover and page design: Nicola Stratford

Notice: This book contains information that is true, complete, and accurate to the best of our knowledge. However, the author and Rourke Publishing LLC offer all recommendations and suggestions without any guarantees and disclaim all liability incurred in connection with the use of this information.

Safety first! Activities appearing or described in this publication may be dangerous. Always work with a trained coach and spotters when learning new cheerleading skills.

Library of Congress Cataloging-in-Publication Data

Maurer, Tracy, 1965-
    Cheerleading practice / Tracy Nelson Maurer.
        p. cm. -- (Jump and shout)
    Summary: "Cheerleaders blend amazing athletic skills and spirited talent to perform breathtaking stunts. They work hard to boost school pride and win over judges at stiff competitions. Coaches expect teamwork, dedication, good grades, and healthy attitudes"--Provided by publisher.
    Includes index.
    ISBN 1-59515-503-1 (hardcover)
    1. Cheerleading--Juvenile literature. I. Title. II. Series.
    LB3635.M27 2006
    791.6'4--dc22
                                2005012717

Printed in the USA

cg/cg

Rourke Publishing
1-800-394-7055
www.rourkepublishing.com
sales@rourkepublishing.com
Post Office Box 3328, Vero Beach, FL 32964

TABLE OF CONTENTS

CHAPTER **1**   READY? OK!..................................5

CHAPTER **2**   INSIDE TRYOUTS............................13

CHAPTER **3**   AGAIN...AND AGAIN!.....................23

CHAPTER **4**   CHEERLEADING EXTRAS 33

CHAPTER **5**   HAPPY CAMPERS 39

FURTHER READING 45

WEB SITES 45

GLOSSARY 46

INDEX 48

Big smiles add to any performance.

Chapter 1

How many long-distance runners have you seen smiling mile after mile? How many soccer players have you seen smiling while they lose a game in the rain?

Among the world's athletes, cheerleaders smile as much as gymnasts and figure skaters do—except cheerleaders also smile before, during, and after they jump, flip, and do the splits. Cheerleaders smile in any weather, hour after hour, win or lose. And cheerleaders' performances aren't complete until the fans smile back.

Here's the fun (and slightly twisted) part: Cheerleaders actually enjoy these physical and mental challenges.

Are *you* ready?

Work Zone Ahead

Some people say cheerleading is a sport. Others claim it's an activity. Either way, cheerleading demands athletic skills, such as strength, **stamina**, flexibility, and coordination. These physical skills don't just happen overnight.

You're going to work your body. Just as you would do before starting any other physically demanding activity (or sport), check with your doctor. Most squads require a physical examination anyway.

Worried about asthma or a disability? Ask your doctor for ideas to help you over those hurdles. With physical therapy, medicine, or other treatment plans—and a healthy dose of willpower, you might be surprised how far you can go!

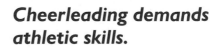

Cheerleading demands athletic skills.

As to ZZZZZZZs

Physically, your growing body needs about seven to ten hours of sleep every night. That's when you heal overworked muscles and fight off infections.

Mentally, your brain needs the downtime to recharge. And you'll want your brain firing at full power when you start memorizing **cheers** and **chants**. More important, a well-rested brain is ready to study. Take your schoolwork seriously! A bad fall can take you out of cheerleading, but nobody can take away what you learn.

You may hear your friends or family say things like, "You're too smart for cheerleading." Cheerleaders with As and Bs on their report cards rewrite the old ditzy **stereotype**. They also stay on the team. Many schools have academic standards for cheerleaders, often requiring a B average.

Studying and practicing take time. **Time-management** skills help you plan for schoolwork, cheerleading, friends, family, and other parts of your life—including sleep.

Pass the test with lots of rest.

Lame rhyme, but it's true. You don't get As without your Zs. Take a nap when you feel run down. Your body tells you when it wants to rest. Listen up!

8

Balancing so many things isn't easy. Ask your parents for ideas. Some schools have guidance counselors who can help you learn about managing your time, too.

Food for Thought

Diet doesn't mean what you *don't* eat. Your diet is really about what you *do* eat. A balanced diet delivers the **nutrients** you need from head to toe.

Proper nutrition is all about making good choices.

Your body and your brain need calories and proteins like a car needs gasoline. Without the right fuel, you can't go far. **Vegetarians** or people who follow a religiously based diet must pay close attention to their foods' nutrients. Ask your parents to help plan weekly meals with you.

❃ Choose fresh fruits and vegetables, low-fat milk and dairy foods, and grilled or baked meats and other protein sources. Instead of empty calories from cookies or chips, munch powerful calories from complex **carbohydrates** in multi-grain breads and cereals.

✿ Eat breakfast. Whine if you must, but eat breakfast. It boosts your brain power and helps stop you from packing in too many calories later in the day.

✿ Keep healthy snacks like cheese sticks or apples in your backpack, especially if there's a long span between a meal and practice.

✿ Drink water regularly throughout the day. Pump more water into your system before and after a workout or cheerleading practice. If you feel thirsty, you're already too low on water.

Better fuel equals better performance. A Daytona racecar needs top-quality gasoline and more of it than even the nicest family-mobile. Cheerleaders burn a lot of calories during practice and performances. You might be hungry more often than even your nicest non-athletic friends.

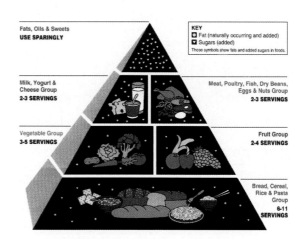

The building blocks of proper nutrition

Stay tuned to your own body, not what other people eat or don't eat. Learn more about nutrition and how it affects you. Eat right and you're good to go!

Trouble Signs

Imagine a driver who steers every conversation toward how much gasoline his nice car burns. He may or may not mention that some days he overfills the tank every ten miles. Or that, on other days, he runs the tank on empty. Secretly, he's worried about how well he drives and if people really like his nice car. His friends only see that his car is ready for a breakdown—a serious no-go that requires a professional mechanic.

See, the real worry isn't about gasoline. And eating disorders aren't about food. People with eating disorders usually need professional help to fix their troubles. If you know someone (or it's you) who talks nonstop about food, eats too much and throws up, or never eats enough, ask an adult for help. Eating disorders can cause lasting body breakdowns and so much worse.

No Nasties!

Nag, nag, nag. Ever notice how parents, teachers, and coaches seem to nag about smoking, alcohol, drugs, and sexually transmitted diseases? Here's an inside tip: It's usually because they care about you.

Nod and agree with them. Play by the rules. Respect yourself. Losing your place on the cheerleading team will be the least of your worries if you mess around with the nasty stuff.

Enough said.

Chapter 2

INSIDE TRYOUTS

Coaches often hold tryouts in the spring for the upcoming school year. Do your homework—not just for classes, but study the cheerleading team, too.

If it's a *competition team*, stunt skills and tumbling moves will rank high during tryouts. Learn which contests the team usually targets. If you're a beginner and the team expects to claim a state title at the advanced level, then you might want to find a different squad.

If it's a *school team*, think about how the school shows spirit. Memorize the school song. Many teams teach routines based on the school song at tryouts. If you already know the tune before tryouts begin, you can focus better on the routine.

A cheer camp is a great place to learn cheerleading skills.

Study the main cheers and chants for your sport. Go to basketball games, if you want to earn a place on the basketball cheerleading squad. Understand the game rules and review the sport's jargon. Would you cheer for a "first-down" in basketball or a "free-throw" in football? Show the coach that you appreciate the sport.

Cheers and Chants

Cheerleaders cheer. They also chant. A cheer is usually longer than a chant, and it has a distinct start and end. The team performs a routine to a cheer, often featuring a stunt—perhaps a jump, pose, or exciting toss. Pre-game and halftime shows, pep rallies, and competitions feature cheers. Chants are usually short, repeated phrases that cheerleaders perform from the sidelines with claps, hand and arm moves, and single jumps.

Practice Time

Most teams invite potential cheerleaders to join special practices before tryouts. Some practices happen just a few hours before tryouts. Others are intense weekend "clinics" designed to teach several **compulsory** skills—the positions, jumps, and tumbling moves required at tryouts.

It helps if you're a fan of the sport you cheer for.

Compulsories vary from school to school and team to team. Tumbling moves borrowed from gymnastics, such as cartwheels and splits, often make the list. Coaches might ask for the herkie, pike, double hook, toe-touch, or other challenging jumps.

Work through the list of compulsory skills, especially jumps, waaaaaaay before the tryouts. Nailing those jumps takes practice, practice, practice.

Cheerleaders combine gymnastics and dance in their routines.

Tryout Tips

- ✿ Arrive early and introduce yourself to others
- ✿ Wear workout clothes: shorts and tucked-in shirt, white socks, gym shoes
- ✿ Take off jewelry, spit out gum, avoid heavy makeup
- ✿ Pull hair back in a ponytail or barrettes
- ✿ Warm up and stretch
- ✿ Smile!

Passing the Tests

Tryouts test your skills, knowledge, attitude, and grace under pressure. The first test might be your grades. Expect to provide your report cards, a doctor's physical examination report, permission forms, and other documents.

"Clinics" prepare you for tryouts.

Coaches often ask a small group of judges—perhaps former cheerleaders, coaches from other schools, or school administrators—to score the tryout performances. Using a point system helps prevent a popularity contest. Usually, candidates with the highest scores fill the open positions on the squad. Coaches make the final decisions.

Some tryouts include face-to-face interviews. The judges want to learn about you. They listen for your **enthusiasm**, honesty, and sincerity. They look for eye contact and comfortable body language. Uncross your arms and keep your hands in your lap or on the table. Fidgety wiggles shake the judges' attention away from you. Stay focused and smile at the end.

Pointers for Points

Judges know you're nervous. They want you to do your best. And they expect that you might do better at some things than others. Listen carefully to their instructions. Ask questions if you're not sure. Take a deep breath before you start. Relax. Give every judge a nice dose of direct eye contact. Then smile and start.

Judges rank how well you demonstrate your skills. They also take note of how you handle yourself when you goof up. Keep going. Keep smiling. Stopping, apologizing, swearing, or crying won't fly. Confidence and **poise** count in your cheers, jumps, stunts, tumbling, and dance. They're important between performances, too.

What Judges Judge

Your Cheer
- Correct and crisp moves
- Memorized words
- Strong voice
- Eye contact
- Smiles

Your Jump
- Form and technique: straight back, proper arm positions, feet together on landings
- Height, flexibility, and control
- Unison movement if performed with other cheerleaders
- Ease and difficulty level
- Smiles

Your stunt

- Safety awareness
- Form, technique, coordination, strength, flexibility, and timing
- Teamwork
- Ease and difficulty level
- Smiles

Your Tumbling

- Willingness to learn
- Coordination, flexibility, strength, and timing
- Form, technique, and ability
- Grace and control
- Smiles

Cheerleaders practice their teamwork.

Your Dance
- ✿ Body expression and eye contact
- ✿ Interaction with audience
- ✿ Correct moves (learned quickly!) and unison movement
- ✿ Rhythm, technique, and timing
- ✿ Smiles

A squad works on moving in unison.

Afterward, smile. Smile until you're home. Then watch a movie or do something to keep your mind off tryouts. Think positive! That's what cheerleaders do. Beating yourself up over mistakes or silly answers wastes your time and energy.

What if you don't make the team? Find ways to stay involved. Work out to build your stamina and flexibility. Take gymnastics or dance classes. Volunteer at cheerleading competitions or help with practices. You'll learn more about the squad, so you're better prepared for tryouts next time.

Every member of the team is expected to be at every practice.

Chapter 3

AGAIN... AND AGAIN!

Cheerleading practices begin soon after the coach selects the team for next year. Practices may last for as long as two hours. You might practice before or after school three or four times each week. Most teams expect you to attend *every* practice. Miss more than two or three practices without a good reason—a really, really good reason—and you could be off the team.

What if you injure yourself—maybe sprain an ankle or wrist— and can't cheer for a while? You still show up for practice.

What if you have a huge algebra test and a report to write for social studies? You still show up for practice.

What if you have your period or your face erupts with volcano-size zits? You guessed it: You still show up for practice.

When you join the team, you agree to commit yourself to the team. You must manage your time to squeeze in all of the practices. You also must stick with the practices, even when you're bored practicing the same cheers over and over and over again…and again. You show your commitment when you work hard at *every* practice.

The Core Four

Like all athletes, cheerleaders condition their bodies by following a training program. Cheerleading training programs use drills, or exercises, to improve the four core areas of physical performance: skill, **cardiovascular** stamina, strength, and flexibility.

Skill

Repeating the same cheer again and again builds your physical skills. To demonstrate your skill, you need to show proper form—the correct body position. You also need to show proper technique— the correct way to move your body.

Sometimes coaches use skill drills to smooth trouble spots or build speed. A favorite motion drill, called "'Til Everyone's Perfect," tests the team's ability to focus and quickly respond in **unison**. For example, everyone stands in a circle facing each other. The coach yells a movement, such as "T arms." Everyone must snap their arms straight out from each side at the same time. The drill repeats until the team snaps into Ts exactly at the same time. Then the coach adds another movement to the T arms and again repeats the drill until everyone's perfect.

Cardiovascular stamina

Cardio means "heart." *Vascular* means "blood system." Cardiovascular, or **aerobic**, exercise revs up your heart rate. As your heart pounds faster, your lungs suck in more air. This pumps more oxygen into your blood system and carries it to the active muscles.

Every practice and every performance begin with stretching exercises.

It helps to have workout partners.

Build your stamina with cardiovascular workouts, such as running, dancing, fast marching, kicking, and waving your arms above your head. Almost all cheerleading practices use aerobic moves to increase your heart and lung power. A strong cardiovascular system helps you finish more cheers without panting like a dog.

Strength

Strength training is **anaerobic**. It's not about increasing your air power. It's about building muscle power. Strength becomes especially important for jumps and stunts, when you pull your body into the air or lift a teammate up high.

Try **plyometric** exercises that use your own body weight for resistance, such as push-ups and sit-ups. Some older high school cheerleaders might be ready to lift weights with help from a coach or trainer.

Watch for proper form with plyometrics or weights. Count your repetitions, or reps. Your coach might say, "Do three reps of twelve." That means do twelve lifts, then briefly rest that muscle with a fifteen-second stretch. Repeat. Stretch. Repeat. Stretch. Just three reps, no more.

A trainer or coach can teach you the right way to lift weights when your body is ready.

When it's too easy, your coach adds weight or increases the plyometric difficulty with a second in-between movement, such as a hand-clap between push-ups.

Plan your anaerobic strength training for days opposite aerobic cheerleading practices. Then work your lower body one day and your upper body on another day. Ask your coach for help creating the right workout for your body.

Flexibility

Gentle muscle stretches improve your flexibility and grace. They also help build strength and prevent injuries.

Warm up and stretch your whole body before you practice or perform. Cool down and stretch again after both.

Your coach probably will use a warm-up routine that begins with light cardiovascular movement for about five or ten minutes, followed by stretching exercises. You might hold some stretches for 10 to 15 seconds. In time, you might hold for 60 seconds.

Breathe deeply while you stretch to bring more oxygen into your body. Don't strain those muscles—just flex until you feel the stretch. Avoid pain. The "no pain, no gain" rule does not apply to cheerleaders.

Stretching increases flexibility.

S-T-R-E-T-C-H Together

Bored with stretching alone? Try partner stretches. They're fun and help build team spirit.

Diamond Straddle

Work on your inner thighs and lower back. Sit on the floor with your back straight and your legs wide apart in a "V." Your partner sits across from you in the same position, touching foot to foot (or foot to ankle). The four legs make a diamond. With straight arms, each partner holds the other person's elbows. Then one partner leans forward as the other leans back. Keep your back straight! Hold the stretch for 10 counts, then lean the opposite way.

Double Ham Stretch

Hamstrings are opposite quadriceps (thigh muscles). Lift one straight leg into the air as you balance on the opposite foot. Your partner holds your heel and gently—GENTLY—raises your outstretched leg. Be sure your back stays straight. Flex your foot toward your forehead. Count to 10. Switch legs. Then switch and hold for your partner.

Stretching beforehand helps prevent injuries during a performance.

Chapter 4

CHEERLEADING EXTRAS

Cheerleading has blossomed with performance flair over the years. Amazing tumbling moves and glitzy dances rock cheerleader routines everywhere—from halftime shows at school football games to competitive cheerleading events.

Tumbling moves, such as cartwheels, handsprings, and other body-flipping moves, often link together in a **tumbling run**. Coaches like to use exciting tumbling runs in their **choreography** to help distract the crowd while the team loads a stunt.

Tumbling moves are attention getters.

Many coaches expect their teams to have tumbling skills from the start. Most cheerleaders take gymnastics classes in addition to their cheering practices. Some gyms or studios offer classes just for cheerleaders. "Cheernastics," or power tumbling, focuses on moves used in cheerleading instead of traditional gymnastic forms.

Safety comes first in tumbling as it does in all of cheerleading. A gymnastics coach should teach the proper form for each move, building a run as the team masters one move at a time.

The gymnastics coach might also assign special exercises that increase flexibility and strength. If you train as a gymnast, plan to spend a lot of time working out. And then expect to spend even more time practicing with your cheerleading squad!

Dancing to the Music

Today's cheerleaders take their positive attitudes beyond the sidelines. From parades and pep rallies to exhibitions and serious contests, cheerleaders now jazz up their performances with music and dance.

Many cheerleading routines use dance moves.

Dancing lets cheerleaders show off their physical conditioning and fine sense of rhythm. Their routines flow smoothly with the music. They use dance skills from hip-hop, ballet, or jazz and mix in a few high Vs or toe-touch jumps, too.

The coach designs the choreography to showcase the team's skills and unique style. A dance routine usually matches the best part of a high-energy tune, especially for competitions. A team might have less than 180 seconds during a contest to score a trophy.

Your squad might choreograph a routine. Experiment! Start by dancing to a few of your favorite songs. No rules. Maybe add some of your favorite cheer positions, tumbling runs, or ballet leaps. You never know what will work until you try. Mostly, keep it fun. That's worth cheering for every time.

Sports? What Sports?

Physical activity, such as cheerleading, helps your body and your mind. Researchers have found links between increased fitness and improved grades, stronger self-esteem, and less interest in drugs and other bad-news choices.

As athletes, cheerleaders enjoy building their fitness levels. They're often interested in physical activities outside of cheerleading, such as running, in-line skating, biking, and swimming. These aerobic sports use large muscle groups and support cheerleading workouts.

Individual sports fit into busy cheerleading schedules better than competitive team sports do.

Cheerleading practices, games, and events leave little time for basketball, volleyball, or other school sport teams. Some coaches simply don't allow you to join other sport teams.

Enjoy Saturday morning hoops with your friends or play volleyball at the beach. You can still play different sports for fun (and fitness!) on your cheerleading off-days.

Stay active even when you're taking a break from cheerleading.

Chapter 5

HAPPY CAMPERS

Hockey season stretches through the winter. Basketball and lacrosse seasons pick up late winter and early spring. Soccer and baseball seasons cover spring and summer months. Football season tackles late summer and autumn.

Cheerleading doesn't have a set season.

Cheerleading tryouts in the spring decide the squads for the next school year. Even if your squad cheers for a sport like basketball that doesn't play games until January, you'll be busy with practices, fundraisers, and special events well before then.

All-star squads focus mainly on competitions, with or without ties to a certain school. All-star teams might host tryouts in the fall, or whenever they develop new competition routines. Then they enter contests and perform shows year round.

Whether you make the all-star team or a school squad, expect to start attending cheerleading practices right away. Weekly practices continue when school lets out for summer vacation.

During the summer months, cheerleaders might take a "vacation" from their regular practices and head off to cheerleading camp. Serious squads may even require you to attend camp to fine-tune your competition routines.

A cheer team takes part in a regional competition.

Worldwide Lessons

You've probably heard of the herkie jump. Did you know Lawrence Herkimer invented it? He also formed the National Cheerleaders Association (NCA) in 1948. The next year, he held the first cheerleading camp for 52 cheerleaders at Sam Houston College. NCA now hosts over 1,100 cheerleading and dance camps in the United States and around the world, including Japan, Germany, England, Puerto Rico, Mexico, and Panama.

An entire team performs a herkie jump.

Today, several promotion businesses and cheerleading associations offer camps, training sessions for coaches, and contests. The Universal Cheerleaders Association, Cheerleaders of America, and the National Cheerleaders Association rank among the largest and best recognized organizations in the world.

Camp Focus

Nearly all camps work on jumps, stunts, chants and cheers, dance, and tumbling. They teach new routines, stress safety, and build teamwork for beginner to advanced cheerleading levels.

Cheerleaders love to perform.

Camp $ecret

Associations don't sponsor camps just for fun—they make money from camps, too. Your expenses might not end with the camp fee. Companies and sponsors at camps sell everything from shoes and T-shirts to **pompons** and hair doodads.

Attending a good cheerleading camp can be a great experience.

Camp programs and costs vary. Look on the Internet or in the back of cheerleading magazines for options. And there are many options: day camps (where you go home at the end of the day), sleep-away camps, two-day camps or three-day camps, or camps that last for a week or more. Some train just for competitions. Others match with certain sports. You'll find camps across the United States and around the world.

Check the camp's safety equipment, training, and history. Look for experienced directors and counselors. They know what triggers you to try harder. They play the right music, arrange special little contests, and plan every activity to help push your skills further.

Don't think you'll wow the counselors the first day (besides, it's their job to wow you!). Counselors expect that your cheers need work. Why else would you go to camp? Listen carefully and work hard. ...Harder. ...Your very hardest. Then you just might amaze them (and yourself) at the end!

Further Reading

Cheerleading in Action by John Crossingham.
  Crabtree Publishing Company, New York, New York, 2003.

Let's Go Team: Cheer, Dance, March / Chants, Cheers, Jumps
  by Craig Peters. Mason Crest Publishers, Philadelphia, 2003.

The Ultimate Guide to Cheerleading by Leslie Wilson.
  Three Rivers Press, New York, New York, 2003.

Web Sites

American Association of Cheerleading Coaches and Advisors
http://www.aacca.org/

CheerHome.com, an online information clearinghouse
http://www.CheerHome.com/

Girls' athletic information, sponsored by the Women's Sports Foundation
http://www.gogirlgo.com

Girls' health information, U.S. Department of Health and Human Services
http://www.girlpower.gov/

Ms. Pineapple's Cheer Page
http://www.mspineapple.com/

National Cheerleaders Association
http://www.nationalspirit.com/

National Council for Spirit Safety & Education
http://www.spiritsafety.com/

United Performing Association, Inc.
http://www.upainc.net/

Universal Cheerleaders Association
http://www.varsity.com

Glossary

aerobic (air OH bik) — in exercises, movement that makes the heart and lungs work harder to pump blood and oxygen to the body

anaerobic (AN uh ROH bik) — in exercises, movement focused on muscle strengthening, not pumping up the heart and lungs

carbohydrates (KAR boh HY drayts) — nutrients from foods such as breads and sugars that provide energy for the body

cardiovascular (KARD ee oh VAS kyoo lur) — the heart and blood, especially as they work with the lungs to supply oxygen to the body

chants (CHANTS) — in cheerleading, the short, repeated singsong phrases often performed on the sidelines in response to big game plays or to fill short pauses in the game action

cheers (CHEERZ) — in cheerleading, the longer phrases that usually rhyme and match with gestures and stunts; cheers distinctly start and end, and often occur during time-outs, halftimes or other longer game breaks or at competitions

choreography (KOR ee OG ruh fee) — the plan or patterns for dance steps, movement, or action, usually set to music

compulsory (KUM pul suh ree) — something that is required

enthusiasm (en THOO zee AZ um) — excitement or lively interest

nutrients (NYU tree unts) — good parts of foods that fuel the body

plyometric (PLY uh MEH trik) — in exercises, movements that use the body's own weight to build strength

poise (POYZ) — grace, self-confidence, unruffled presence

pompons (POM ponz) — in cheerleading, the tufted accessories used to add movement, color, and sound to performances; some dictionaries also use pompom or pom-pom

stamina (STAM uh nuh) — strength and power to keep going, to continue

stereotype (STAIR ee oh TYP) — right or wrong, a commonly believed and simple image or idea about a group of people

time-management (TYM MAN ij munt) — fitting activities into a schedule

tumbling run (TUM bling RUN) — two or more tumbling moves, such as cartwheels or handsprings, performed immediately one after the other

unison (YOO nuh sun) — something done the same way at the same time

vegetarians (VEJ uh TARE ee unz) — people who do not eat meat, fish, or fowl, and sometimes also food that comes from animals, such as milk and eggs

Index

all-star team   39, 40
brain   8, 9, 10
camp   40, 41, 42, 43, 44
Cheerleaders of America   42
compulsory skills   15, 16
dance   19, 20, 21, 33, 35, 36, 37, 42
diet   9, 10
eating disorders   11
exercise   24, 25, 27, 29
fitness   38
gymnastics   16, 21, 35
Herkimer, Lawrence   41

judges   18, 19
National Cheerleaders Association (NCA)   41, 42
nutrients   9
safety   20, 35, 42, 44
sleep   8
stereotype   8
stretching   16, 27, 29, 31
time-management   8
tryouts   13, 15, 16, 17, 18, 21, 39
Universal Cheerleaders Association (UCA)   42

About The Author

Tracy Nelson Maurer specializes in nonfiction and business writing. Her most recently published children's books include the *Roaring Rides* series, also from Rourke Publishing LLC. Tracy lives near Minneapolis, Minnesota with her husband Mike and their two children.